Dougie's Ton

& 99 Other Sonnets

T0363967

We'll build in sonnets pretty roomes;
As well a well wrought urn becomes
The greatest ashes, as half-acre tombes,
And by those hymnes, all shall approve
Us Canoniz'd for Love:

JOHN DONNE

I made a map of the island, it was elaborately
and (I thought) beautifully coloured …
it contained harbours that pleased me like sonnets …

ROBERT LOUIS STEVENSON

Dougie's Ton

& 99 Other Sonnets

Syd Harrex

LYTHRUM PRESS

ADELAIDE

First published by
Lythrum Press
PO Box 243 Rundle Mall
Adelaide
South Australia 5000

www.lythrumpress.com.au

December 2007

Cover graphic: based on a photograph by Patrick Eagar
Designed and typeset in Giovanni 10/18 by Michael Deves
Printed and bound by Hyde Park Press, Adelaide

ISBN 978 1 921013 16 4

This project has been assisted by the Australian Government through the
Australia Council, its arts funding and advisory body.

Contents

'Bard-Birth' 1

Our Mutual Mentor 2

Man-made Gods 3

Feather on Foolscap 4

Sea Eagles 5

Self-deception 6

A Gentle Huntsman 7

Late Day 8

Private Eye 9

Song-line from Penneshaw 10

Oceanic Abstract 11

Terms and Conditions 12

'Do Not Use this Urinal: Leaking through the Roof' 13

Full Moon at 5 A.M. 14

Two in One Morning 15

Som's Party 16

Biopsy 17

The Heritage Equation 18

Aperture 19

Happy Ending 20

Brushing the Canvas 21

Drops of Water 22

Gravitation and the Speed of Light 23

Love 24

The Last Knob of Blue 25

Neither Serpent Nor Rope 26

Was it a Celica? 27

Corner Shop 28

Valediction 29

Why? 30

Port Arthur 31

Meeting a Traveller from an Antique Land 32

Changing Tenses   33
Spring's Ingenious Augury: Ada to Rick   34
Romantic Agony   35
Homage to Frailty   36
Wisteria   37
In the Wake of Abel Jans Tasman   38
Aroma Therapy   39
Retirement Issues   40
'Wild thyme and the gadding vine'   41
Reconciliation   42
Holofernes Stiff on Night-Watch   43
Friend from Bangalore   44
A Newcastle Wild Coole Swan   45
The 'You' in All of Us   46
Rear Window   47
Comedy   48
Covenant   49
Dawn Chorus Republic   50
Time's Timeless Art   51
Haute Cuisine   52
Surviving Clichés   53
Silk   54
Laughter   55
Teething Time   56
We are Reminded   57
Demonising the Other   58
Biting the Apple   59
Anancy's Old Come-on Extravaganza   60
À la Proust   61
Letting the Dog Back In   62
Fellow Traveller   63
Immobilised by the Mobile   64
Job Interview   65
Junior Mateship   66
Aberrations   67

Summer Equinox	68
Overcast Day	69
Hyphenation, or 'Only connect'	70
Mirror Image	71
Just Desserts	72
Affairs of the Blood	73
The Pilgrim has a Glimmer or Two of Enlightenment	74
Beach Gallops: Stanley, Tasmania	75
Our National Game	76
Winter's Tale	77
Ode and Urn	78
A Rain Canticle	79
Romance	80
Fencing Metaphor	81
Dear Will,	82
Bringing a Book to Life	83
Time Warp	84
No Sweat!	85
Scumbag in Uniform	86
Oedipus but not Rex	87
The Ocean Child in Hobart Town, 1844	88
I Get a Kick Out of You	89
Creative Writing Gathering Hastings Bay (28.01.07)	90
From Penneshaw at Midnight	91
The Best is Yet to Come	92
Triangles in the Sky	93
Out There	94
Five Sonnets for Vincent O'Sullivan (from *Rites of Spring*)	
Poetry Interruptus	95
'Not what skeletons think about'	96
On re-reading O'Sullivan's essay on Gwen Harwood	97
On re-reading Gwen Harwood's *The Lion's Bride*	98
Encore	99
Dougie's Ton	100

Acknowledgements

Some of the sonnets were first published in the following periodicals and books: *Australian Letters, Island, Span, Weekend Australian, Westerly, Alas for the Pelicans!* (Adelaide: Wakefield Press, 2002), *Towards a Transcultural Future* (NY: Rodopi, 2002), *Still Shines When You Think of It* (Wellington: Victoria University Press, 2007).

I am deeply indebted to Michael Deves for his encouragement patience and professional standards; to Sudesh Mishra for his sifting and editing expertise; to Tully Barnett and Melinda Graefe for their discriminating and professional conversion of manuscript to typescript; and to David 'Digger' Agnew for what became a long-term loan of the cricket books cited on page 100.

S.H.

for

Jane, Jaime, Sudesh

'Bard-Birth'

(for Ken Arvidson who invented that term on awakening to ecstatic noise in the bird-bath outside his bedroom window in Adelaide, a far time ago)

The past incorrigibly iambic,
Eros spawns your sonnets with felt-tipped tongue
to suit your pumping lines, yet when you're hot
rules are there to crunch between trochee thighs
so readers can mould simulacrum truths
into things of beauty . This is the way
a love play, out of sorts with death, makes good
the sad business of lost brotherhood.
From your example we learn the salving
art of redressing errors so they seem
not to have happened; magical logic
that cossets candle flames against the draught
with firefly phosphorescence in a glass
luminously, as fitful shadows pass.

Our Mutual Mentor

(for Graeme Hetherington)

Some nights he acceded to the old moon's
despair, but never to flinch, to be wrong
or heretical in clairvoyant song.
Art always his mistress, his monsoonal
'only connect' principle—Faustus's fear
and trembling with Spenser's epic spirit;
Keats's urn of truth and beauty with Trakl's
'red foliage full of guitars'; the young but
doomed Malley's duelling banjo voices.
Wily advocate of the safety net,
his lessons—master metaphors for life—
never simplified ambiguities.
Nor did his devious chuckle, his lark-
swift wit, while we just hovered in the dark.

Man-made Gods

No god made by man equips my spirit
for the promised flight. Woman may do better.
Freight of fear, grief of guilt, coiled passion—
our vehicles have not proved space-worthy.
Those who have met the son of god made by
man move in exalted inner circles,
but is their mystery more than ego,
superfluous in the endless outerness
where the migration of the birds, the Milky
Way, the logic of conception, being
born, dying, are sufficiently miraculous
for imaginations starved of dream substance?
So enough of priests and their big spending;
I'll put my faith in a feminine ending.

Feather on Foolscap

On the back of a foolscap envelope
I draw an oriel for no good reason
(an echo from childhood perhaps); green door
threshold into a fourth dimension.
But my high window squats shut, so with brisk
lines I open it to the firmament,
close my eyes, and sense a starlit mist settle
on my face, induced by ripples of air.
No one's permission but mine, so it seemed,
was needed to enter this embrasure,
for here were time and space I wholly dreamed
subject to instant birth or erasure.
I thought I saw an osprey up-lift in
and find on my sketch a featherish fin.

Sea Eagles

(Section H, Hundred of Menzies, Kangaroo Island)

The man-sized nest is a grey cone upside-
down, swelling in the eucalyptus fork
year by year. Eagle excrement excellent
mortar, feathers waxed eiderdown; the walls
wicker-woven stuff of generations.
That discipline teaches us how to spy
and pry in silence (unlike gutter journalists) at a courteous
distance. Hence an unpredictable reward
awaits you one unchosen day: a rising
as from a grave, a slow-motion fusion
of lift-off flux into palpable air,
and then the gully glide beyond tree time
to the sea of feasting. Effortless grace,
couplet-winged, diving down through serene space.

Self-deception

'I don't look older. The young grow younger.
I read this truth in other eyes as well.
I'm sure you recognised yourself, my friend,
in what I'm saying saying cannot tell.'
'You don't look younger. The young grow older.
Generation exacts the price of bones
which is the urge to quit the sheath of flesh,
and envy spirit in the simple stones.'
There we have it: loud and clear as winter.
The only position's opposition.
Sky without cloud, wind, sun is not weather …
and erode we shall into extinction,
though star says to moon, and grass to boulder:
The young grow younger. I don't look older.

A Gentle Huntsman

A spider trespassed in my sleep, fell on
my face (for so my dream intelligence
construed—I confused by its soft brush-strokes
like a kiss which might have been my lover's).
My impulse to hit, yet not my instinct,
was mean and wrong, like the paranoia
trap, a deadly game of hysteria:
the black widow's lust in her web of hate.
If it's spider myths we need, Africa's
anarchy god—Anancy—is just fine.
But my visitant was neither ogre
nor hero; only the gentle Huntsman
who shared a corner of the lonely room
when childhood was speechless and all was gloom.

Late Day

Late afternoon light is jam on butter.
No wonder sugar ants are still drilling
at this crystal hour when dust is dancing
with gypsy moths in tatting spiderwebs.
Thrushes flip and dive like agitated
tea-leaves in a glass silver-lidded pot.
Ochre autumn powders creek-bed and rock;
citrus mist smudges hillside eucalypts.
The gully breeze vibrates a wind-chime's pipes;
mixed scents from confetti garden beds drift
by as sunset wraps you in sari silk
and paints memories into faint corners.
Time is hesitant with a fond lament
for this late day's last will and testament.

Private Eye

High window, low watcher, salacious drama:
it's a plot idea Eye can't dispel now
as sleuthing rain ranges in revealing
Marlow (Chandler's gaberdined, not Conrad's
in thick navy blue) as mansion lights blur
like crumpled trouser-creases, blouse polka
dots. Eye tries to recall a frame recalled
somewhere before. Was it Bogie 'n' Bacall
after the War at the flicks in The Hall
where he learned Badminton and how to give
a Best Man speech? Or just a varnished
print on video; freckle grains and blurred flesh
of lips: Flash-point kiss, apocalypse? …
While Private Eye dissembles out of sight ….

Song-line from Penneshaw

Gales off the ocean unscab the shore-line;
troubles are in the air and in the heart.
Gulls give up gliding, a ferry rocks in
late. This is not the day to read your palm
or mine, nor to play Russian Roulette with
Eros. Our cottage must ride out the storm
blast exultant with divine comedy,
calling forth the sins of humanity.
Neither cowardice nor white-flag surrender
are the ways to go. Instead we must tend
each other's wounds tenderly, ache cuddling
ache, and chord by chord build a bright new shrine
so the song that's yours is equally mine.

Oceanic Abstract

Along the tide-rummaged shore and shunting
sea where gales knife gulls and paw at the dunes'
grasses and vagrant papers, afternoon's
light has the thickness of a crust and waves
frosted solidity.

                    Foam shavings flake
from the rusted bows of a smoke-crunching
steamer and winged appetites in its wake
chop at port-hole scraps like sickles and staves.

Distance, which deducts fastidiously
time from space and each beak-serrated cry
from sound, is the eye's scavenger: the rife
birds look like flies furrowing in offal,
and no conceit of vision can conceal
the parasitic strategies of life.

Terms and Conditions

Section I/O/U

Subrogation: a new clause which describes
what occurs when Cardmembers get sullied
goods from Merchants who have subsequently
gone spunkrupt and not honoured their services.
In these cases the subrogation clause
does not include prelapsarian contracts
with the Merchant Maker who authorised
terms and conditions of the credit card.
As you read these gilt-edged regulations
please remember that the words 'you' and 'your'
mean the person named on the Paradise
Card, and the words 'we', 'our' and 'us' refer
to *Sacramental Express*. Don't be damned,
Please Consider: credit is yours on demand.

'Do Not Use this Urinal: Leaking through the Roof'

That's what the sign said in wobbling letters
on the pub wall. 'Pessimist's Paradise'—
that's what you said as we talked world affairs
descending from one despair to the next,
then silence. An OUT OF ORDER juke box
in one corner sheds its memories of
Put your sweet lips a little closer to
the phone, let's pretend that we're together
all alone back to an antennae time
of the sentiment and mush Innocence
was made on, and film-star melancholy
was to die for in *East of Eden* style.
Gone the gaberdine mystic decadence
superseded by the cynic's commonsense.

Full Moon at 5 A.M.

This declaration of independence,
our moon inventing dawn in the sun's place
in this phosphorescent room, opens eyes
to the milkiness, the translucence, of
things, just as a marauding koala grunts
like a wild pig and infiltrates the silk-
painting dreams in a baby's basinet.
That's when the redeemer arrives to pay
surreptitious court, a pack of cards stacked
in his breast pocket. Will he cut then deal
sacramental Hearts to save innocence
from life's Clubs and Spades, from market-place
chicanery? And will his stake of Diamonds
keep love's lily afloat on moonglow ponds?

Two in One Morning

(*In memory of* P.B. *and* J.C.H.)

Our grapevine transmission is still around,
but slower than it used to be. Does that
mean, however, this's one of its better
mornings?—bringing news through chance encounters
(three hours apart) of the deaths of two mates
from a distant decade? Eighteen months dead,
and four weeks dead, respectively: so too
too late to repair my heart's negligence
and make such amends as friendship's fabric
(despite the threadbare tear, its tattered trust)
will allow. Does our grapevine have a cure
for such ancient remorse for broken ties?
Or just the exotic corpse of a bunch
of shiraz or riesling striped wasps gorge for lunch?

Som's Party

Soft parchment of a face, youth's manuscript
of sooth-spoken stories, legends of long
indeed ago, we ask this shallow favour:
sing one or two of your Bollywood songs,
and if you oblige, smiles will open eyes
and a conjugal chattering will clap
your music rising out of river mists;
out of the rushes of egret wishes.
The world is a lake of fire, of green verbs.
The nouns of time flick and softly stitch such
seconds as are forgotten in the hills
brocaded with the fruits of paradise
as if the indentured labourer's songs
would fill the bowls with rice and right the wrongs.

Biopsy

Cells ignite themselves. Tissue can't resist.
It makes no sense really, but it happens,
casual as campfires which never die
content to be ash. You wonder about
God's commands and those who kneel before them.
For me, that Faith which justifies the evils
of crazed believers I spit out like phlegm.
I'm a metaphysical pragmatist.
It's all show and bust this cosmos of ours.
You spin the wheel, grab first or second prize
(one day a chicken, one night a crayfish),
yet the last message says you cannot win.
And I must lose all my friends who have died;
here within, and there on the other side.

The Heritage Equation

A child picks up anything—a spiral
on a beach or pine-cone among needles
and examines it fist to palm the size
of a small mushroom (humid vegetable,
cream, pink and dark sepia, wild or garden;
vaginal). The action is the word. So
too, in lateral time, does the child
drop a pebble in a pool adults name
the psyche. Thus the law of gravity
crosses laser beams with flights of memory,
and the effort to name a bird before
it's dissolved by cloud will delight the child
who with shell and cone, sea and sour-sob strands
transfers these deeds into the parents' hands.

Aperture

Today the boy lost his first tooth while
playing football at Recess but found it
in Jurassic grass, like a single grain
of rice, before a magpie got there first.
So all was cool. Teacher-wrapped in tissue,
this reverenced bone travelled home first-class;
a leprechaun baby in a hearse pod.
O grand epic, Lilliputian indeed!
But then with chit of deconstruction
the child played his parents and their accounts
like figures in a pack of cards, and wrote:
'Dear God Ferry Please leave too dollers
and don't take my tooth'. The going-rate these days
for making make-believe myth pay both ways.

Happy Ending

Tonight a few more stars disintegrate
in posthumous fluorescence of their fate.
The moon of Eros has a pitted face
it tries to hide behind a scarf of lace,
a millennium after Cleopatra
went Cydnus sailing and Antony spat the
dummy. Moor Othello fared no better
from jealous Law and its envious Letter.
Juliet Capulet and Romeo
Montagu (whose star sign was hirsute Leo)
were mis-managed by their agents. You know
the rest, you say; their tryst on Death's pillow.
But that's not all. Their cover's blown; no doubt!
As she died Juliet pushed a foetus out.

Brushing the Canvas

(for Tom)

The helicopter flies in paranoid
circles above the sandwich wrappers thrust
and thrown about like ravenous seagulls
by the out-door Student Set between 1
and 2, though it is always luncheon time
on the grass; the women elegantly
apparelled in crinoline and cream lace,
the men naked apart from beards, condoms,
and one or two daisy accessories.
I watch Gleghorn painting these spiral models
expecting *à la Manet*, but instead
witness an annihilation of forms
until only his colours, the earth like a cloud,
copulate; granulating in a shroud.

Drops of Water

Guitars began as sun-forest music.
Their plankton rite of passage to the bush
ballad was a butterfly progression,
folkloric yolk-lyric in the hills' mist,
snake-slithering concerto burns and creeks,
hallowe'ening o'er sand-budging slipstreams,
pebble breasts, rococo anthems, a cliff
quietus gorge where a wedge-tail eagle
becomes the plectrum of the tidal air
creating a corroboree of she-oaks
where there is no need for cathedrals.
Dreamtime's a spiderweb continuum:
ghosts of the ear, wild-flowers of the throat;
summer tide of pure song, inside, remote.

Gravitation and
the Speed of Light

We try to understand the principles
of fallen matter (like a Granny Smith
in sour grass), and the reasons why a star
seen across our night was a Phoebus death
aeons ago. Makes you think, doesn't it?
Looking out to sea from a shifting shore,
or up from cliffs at candelabra skies:
how we are falsified in our own eyes.
Such huge issues, old elusive clues—those
are the ghosts imprinted in the tissue
paper of flesh's hypothetical souls.
Falling, sunlight in your brain, there's this:
something in your childhood that understood,
permitted fruit to blossom forth from wood.

Love

Like the earth it is always there, but like
the moon eventually, yes, yes it will
disappear with the consequence that one
morning when you wake under languid sheets
there will be different scents in the air:
neither lemon of the moon nor orange
of the sun to distribute their hive-waxed
hues in the sunrooms of your sonnets.
So when you watch the shooting stars dissolve
in the black velvet of the sky, and when
you separate dust and tears from your eye,
the confrontation of this life and death
is visibly syphoned into that clone
which is the last song singing in your bone.

The Last Knob of Blue

... everything had to balance 'down to the last ha'penny and the last knob of blue', as my mother used to say.
(*Elsie Stokie*, A Life Together, A Life Apart)

Childhood. When time was vertical. We lived
by the sea under a mountain that loomed
through all the weathers, in pitch darknesses
of my dreams instead of God. Its snow-line
was heaven-high above our swimming days,
but in the winter mist of skeletons—
of sleet and hail and drilling rains, of snow
gathering in powdery moonlight—no
margins could be relied on. I wondered
what it would be like to die, unconsoled
by legends of the Cross. But when I lit
wet kindling under the copper, and watched
my mother swish the cube of blue and stir
the washing, dying was just a starched blur.

Neither Serpent nor Rope

Not for us mesmerism of languages,
of small hills of huge boulders on ochre
open to the eye, untranslatable
to our vibrating ears: so strange the taste,
yet so familiar the congestion
in the lungs of insight, these sweating pores.
There's some pinch of suffering one adores
like a despicable banquet that finds
you out here; there's an egret on the back
of a buffalo like a direction sign
in a commonplace book: the lapsing, long
silver way Caritas superintends.
What is love if it cannot make amends.

Was it a Celica?

Car screeches, ribald tyres with cliché treads.
Clarinet horn like a full-blast full-stop
in a symphony. Crimson and sporty—
coupé style—abrupt as a blood letting.
Her jeans strenuous in the driver's seat
were flower crusted across ragged holes
like war decorations. Hi, you both cry,
while arthritic traffic is backing up.
There's no time for more than good-will kisses,
Xmas card smiles, for those lipstick complex
questions like who are you at the day's end
of your journey, the dew moment when you
open the front door of your recent past,
and an intimate stranger greets you, at last?

Corner Shop

What childhood didn't have the corner shop,
the store where dreams are bottled, where round sweets
of life are clean and costed under glass,
where gifts of kindness shine on several shelves?
Where society observes the time and taste
of custom, and old and young stimulate
their appetite for quite accustomed love,
and families gather for the Christmas farce?
How familiar, how sickly similar
it is—the epiphany of growing up;
how Moravian the white pavlova
in bridal fruit and cream. My stomach churns
in the mix-master of memory's slop
as if at last it's time to shut up shop.

Valediction

There were always shadows over childhood
slanting like cancers across the graveyard
grass, so don't be frozen by the white shades
of phantom farewell when separation
happens (as it did this morning briskly,
efficiently, in the kitchen of love).
You must amaze your travels with questions
and sea-saw answers only you supply.
Knowing this, your itinerary may pain
me like the vacant pillow by my head,
yet is no worse than a wave crashing on
a boring shore. Eat a hearty repast,
and when the tumult of our son's feeding
time is soaked in sleep, just hold me: first, last.

Why?

This of all questions, the persistent toddler's,
the ancient pursuit of the modern mind
that summons less knowledge than it infers,
the bewildered cry of the maimed and blind,
the death rattle stuck in the feeble throat
when the maker fails to return the call,
the clicking of catechisms learned by rote:
this the most perennial *Why* of all.
A word too hard for word, number, or sign
to render redundant, explain away,
a voice too susceptible to decline,
a mark to start and end every day.
I shrug my heart, retaliate with hot
and cold passion and say to *Why*; 'Why not?'

Port Arthur

Which of my ancestors who grossed the earth,
planted vegetables and vine-bedecked
them with fruits timorous and edenic,
might have dreamed me during their labours?
After their looms were cobwebbed, farms destroyed,
when engine dinosaurs devoured their fields,
what use then, forgiving the sins of others?
What Caritas from Cain's line of brothers?
But convict time aborts my questions in
the uterus of family history,
and shredder death's bureaucracy
eviscerates the hymn of parchment stone.
Restored facades ingratiate the past
With swindles of honey light. The crimes last.

Meeting a Traveller from an Antique Land

'Prayer, women and perfume are pleasing
to me', he said, and I took him at face
value as furnaced sandstorms cowling us
made it difficult to read his eyes, touch
his words, or ply the difference between
breath and beard despite ivory signposts
of teeth. So much for face-value, knowing
when you can't hold an insensate candle
to a pure tongue or soul inscrutable.
So much for so little, I thought, until
the traveller coughed, spat spittle skywards,
and asked me those terrifying questions
your dreams try to smother with cartoon
fictions: your arms trembling, clutching at the moon.

Changing Tenses

He's a humble, awkward, shambling guy
with the feint of a hullo in his eye.

He was the first to dispute the bully's
right to embarrass the poor ones to please

the strong, whose bread rolls oozing vegemite
left in no doubt who'd win the playground fight.

He's like a kitten in a crib, his last
tobacco ashes floating on his past.

As I pay my respects now to the ghost
in the coffin, listen to the last post

tremoring along the vines like autumn
counting the cost of summer, the gross sum,

I see him the other side of my eye:
a brief shadow in the light passing by.

Spring's Ingenious Augury:
Ada to Rick

Dear Grandad, I am scrutinising you

as I imagine you to be, even

as I arrive and before you set eyes

on me. I see I will fathom gentle

curves when at last I make you out, the milk

crib smell new to me but familiar

to you, oh monument of experience

who will always revere me as I once

was inside the bundle in your woollen

arms. Please teach me, too, how to twitch the rod

above the trembling waters, how to reel

the catch in and bless it with a gestured

kiss. Regeneration is time's invader

you shall welcome home with smiles. Love Ada.

Romantic Agony

Incontinent clouds dispense a shower
which fractures light, and mist is gathering
almost-forgotten love in a woman's
eyes, her lavender smiles about to be
smudged, and her eye-lashes webbed by the silk
skeins of sorrow mirroring lost rainbows
in the raiments of love's old sweet song. Yet
again it is the saddest story, it's
melancholy like chimes at midnight
when only frosts can bestow on a ghost
a mantel shape, while in cloistered bed
the woman of the romantic poet's
dreams makes love luxuriously to one
more like his father or his wayward son.

Homage to Frailty

You donate a pad but forget the page
scribbled in your mind. You bestow a pen
but the nib is broken. You bequeath ink
yet it is solid like drought in a creek.
Our best illuminations are hand-prints
hot in side-ways sands that mesmerise
those historians who horizontally
fake truth that's essentially vertical
but which gravity-wise is the lament
that's drifting down here in the moon's bedrooms,
lamp-lighting next-door insects inside your
dreams; your fears, about time present, time past.
So let your heart write it down, almost blind,
while your reason is making up its mind.

Wisteria

Why do I smell and think wisteria
when my cognitive self is afloat on
rivers of remembrance riding childhood's
raft in awe of Huckleberry Finn? How
does such pubescent magic sustain its
silken potency in the throbbing dusk
of time and the quicksilver moonlight on
our ocean's horizon beneath the reefs
of the Milky Way? Maybe if I pick
a page at random in some leather-bound
book of revelations a sign will be
forthcoming: 'thou will compass me about
with songs of deliverance'. Forgotten
responsibilities duly forgiven …

In the Wake of Abel Jans Tasman

(for Graham Tulloch)

I don't wish to fly-cast lake rivers all
these days, nor snatch and patch eddy patterns
(their shimmers glycerine, their shadows calm)
in search of the stream's love-hatching surfaces.
I want to be boy again with willow rod,
worm-baited hook, endangering fishes
of men lipping the meniscus margins
of forbidden knowledge. Now, overblown,
I want to summersalt back to gardens
of the real, poetries of stone and sun …
but that was blue gum eye-inches ago
before the slaughter of the tall timbers
and my treasure island south of Bass Strait
revealed evil reminders of Hell's Gate.

Aroma Therapy

At Pondicherry Bengal jaded seas
counteract a sacred mass of land. Wide
boulevards make for leisurely walk ways
as if in and out of transparencies
tapestried with canker tracks, while ashram
renunciation whites out cute café
society. I munch croissants and say
to myself the French were no worse a sham
than Clive and Macaulay manufactured,
and what's more they left behind grace and taste
which tart British tea and chota pegs could
not quite eliminate. For Room Service
is still a bouquet of tissue language:
'bonjour', 'merci', alive on the tongue's page.

Retirement Issues

(for Elizabeth Close)

You create a theatre of commonsense
—neither of the absurd nor too well made—
in which there's a tightrope reformer's skill
in a multi-lingual eucalyptus shade
where friends are reminded of what you feel
in secrecy of silence, bird watching
when light is shivering with codes
of dusk and dawn, seance of flute and rain.
And you are remindful of in-between
times, of the ghosts of Andrew Marvell's lines
Annihilating all that's made To a
green thought in a green shade. And yea:
reticence of one type of the Other;
jubilation of a rich departure.

'Wild thyme and the gadding vine'

(I.M. *Robin Eaden and Tim Mares*)

We live in an era of departures
and the ghost mystique of saying goodbye.
We lock our memories in a diary den
waiting for a trapped moth to fly again.
We are too gentle to be violent
but there's hurting in our eyes coverlets
cannot hide from the moon's insistence,
reconnoitering the bedrooms where what
happened happened, and where the guiling game
was camouflaged by cereal etiquette
at the breakfast table, when the pet cat
licked the creamy remnants from the chipped bowl.
All we know, each new morning, is that light
which glows inside the lasting heart's secret night.

Reconciliation

First move is to tell the lie as it was,
the harder path of truth, not God-given.
Evil interrogated is a book
that's never closed, a discourse of failed hopes,
of psychiatric fears, of cups of tea.
Story of our world, or so we are told.
Doesn't fit, though, with infants playing
in a sunlit park, mothers knitting shawls,
and black and pale shadows sharing the source
of each other's light. Does not agree with love
catalogued in gold print, framed with silver,
the domestic repertoire. That is why
you don't finish the cross-word puzzle, nor
see in the hanging tree truth's sheer terror.

Holofernes Stiff on Night Watch

I watch him at the cleavage vantage point
at the top of the stairwell where, below,
summer bodices embrace and defy
gravity in a see-through Dantesque
way: Holofernes with a Van Dyke beard,
his eyes curdling with a Yes and a No
of carnal duress. He's wearing a suede
smoking jacket. Tucked in his breast pocket
is a classic play about jealousy
marked with erudite emendations on
such themes as Incest and Fellatio
tongue-wet pencilled in with a jerking hand
in his Nonesuch edition (Immaculate
Perception Series) of *The Devil's Gait*.

Friend from Bangalore

(*for Raj Huilgol*)

Whenever I slump into misanthrope
mood I think of my friend from Bangalore
who once told me parables using Salt
and Pepper shakers. I can't remember
the plot or the allegory, the characters'
forensics, save one was white, the other
black to start with until bleached to summer
tan; but I can recall the big moral.
It had to do with war, and the hour before
battle, and what's the difference between
crimson Agincourt and Kurukshetra,
or Falstaff falsifying Pandava
horoscopes? What's the true business of strife?
Ultimately this: there's more to death than life.

A Newcastle Wild Coole Swan

In memory of Anna Rutherford
(1932–2001)

Lovers must search love's faces, find phrases
to accompany the silent languages
of glances, smiling innuendos, sheer breath.
They need to track paw-prints in snow-fall fields,
navigate drifting shallows of the heart
and bush interiors; then, dusk to dawn,
drift in with the sun to a morning room
where slumber sculptures a tortoise-shell cat.
The rest of the story is memorable
for love's limits, normal forgetfulness:
dream roses residual on pillows,
super-whiz juicing breakfast oranges,
croissants, ground coffee-beans and jersey milk
while morning unfolds like a roll of silk.

The 'You' in All of Us

Entrusting light to language, the star's rose,
you break an egg of speech for a moss man
on the other cliff of abyss—that bourn
from which sunglassed travellers with guide-books
return in droves to rot in paradise.
But you, microscopic, find manuscripts
of lost and found love, forgotten parchment
proofs (wine-cellared and attic-silenced); dry
sepia-invaded photographs sly
as cancer, instantaneous as bliss.
What you say about Marlowe's tapestry
of clichés sets the clock ticking backwards
when time is a blood-loss song of the lark
and hands clutch each other's hopes in the dark.

Rear Window

There's a window opposite mine. I watch
for signs. The first are mere finger fragments
feeling something like an ear. Next the hand
in view rises to reveal a green cup;
some sand-grain freckles and a turquoise ring.
I can almost smell her nail paint. Just been
brushed on I'd say, judging by the wet gloss
look. Now I suss what's going on inside.
Like a Medici painter I have known
you through spy-lascivious binoculars
and a special talent—telepathy!
Like a poet sniffing silk lingerie
for inspiration, I've sniffed out your life.
I am the Insurrection and the Knife.

Comedy

as Shakespeare said, is foolish being wise.
Its wit's the staple diet of good dining,
ricocheting burgundy merriment
from goblet to bowl. It is unerring
in exposing weakness, the noble grail
attempts of Physics and religious sects
to solve the mysteries of the universe:
precocious lyrics lost inside their verse.
Comedy is song and wrong, fits and starts,
the giant's cradle of human behaviour
where madmen reassemble random parts
to the arch amusement of our Saviour.
After such huge mischief, its moral end
(order's all), is illusion round the bend?

Covenant

Charitable seems the august lantern
glow at first light and smoke-grey close of day,
these being the innate peripheries
of love in our almost pastoral world;
our enclosing yet unfolding routine
punctual as the pruned roses' season;
conceptions immaculate as the flight
of charcoal wings across Pelican Lagoon.
For these are the extremes, true and proven,
that issue soft declarations of bliss
and healing reverie: this breakfast fact
of bedroom service, this auspicious way
to get morning started. Coffee, fruit, fresh juice;
and swooping, a winged messenger of truce.

Dawn Chorus Republic

Their majesties of insignificance
are breath-taking to behold. Call us Out
of Tune if you must in this dour as dust
reactionary age which vilifies
radical spirits, forgetting that fires
which keep flesh intact (the blood's hot drumbeat,
this love that makes a house of photographs
keep lost lives alive) are the burning bush's
omniscient gift. Watch ants congregate;
listen to the spree of ecstasy out
of tiny tongue-alliterative throats
invisible in trees. Make the new day
surprise, and your decline's of no concern
if life itself has something new to learn.

Time's Timeless Art

So perfectly lazy is this windless
honey-smooth winter's room that the crows' cries,
normally belligerent as saw screams
in a mill, are slipper-quiet like slow
motion images in a sky-blue day-
dream when the most leisureful place on earth
is the Australian bush; its charade
silences, its bird palpitations, the
insect treks like corpuscles through the veins,
delivering a solace message short
as a telegram used to be, yet long
as ancient day or night in a haiku
read in the glow of a full moon, and rain
splintered sun-signs, hieroglyphed in stone.

Haute Cuisine

With sky and sunset assistance rain nails
mahogany light in place. There are snails
unscrolling the patience of slime, film-shelled
beneath the boot soles of the holocaust
which splash them to soup because sadism's
cheap. Not so palate pleasures; sliding in
erotic oysters, garlic escargot
with diaphanous sauce. If cannibals
had published their recipes what proof would
we have that their chiefs were master gourmets
who created entrees gods would die for?
When I rest a starched napkin on my lap
these days I think about their expedients,
and the history of rare ingredients.

Surviving Clichés

Some simple words refuse to serve our needs
without banality, while true and tried
experience decays to platitudes.
So we survey scant objects in our lives—
the dance of dust in a shaft of sunlight,
the joy of disarray in a child's room—
to express the potency of loving's shroud:
what, too often, we dare not say aloud.
For passion is articulate reticence
as much as clamour; sexual splendour
adulterates madness with common sense,
like the orchid's camouflage of candour.
Our sonnet is the Eagle and the Dove,
the octave swoop, the soft sestet of Love.

Silk

Think of *silk*. A sensuous word esteemed
in Law and golden treasuries of verse;
sign of all avarice of which men dreamed;
dignified inlay for coffin and hearse.
Handmaid of history: the pageant Knights
on Crusade, battle banners of Agincourt;
Samarkand, Marco Polo, sperm-trade rights;
inventory of plunder, imperial gore.
Think again. Now of silk makers. Worms
and vegetarian villagers beside
mud ochre huts on sacramental terms.
Saris of India, the elephant ride.
Spun by women for women, silk is best
simply flowing across a heaving breast.

Laughter

is radical noise. Its rule is to break
all rules, with welcome venom if need be.
It is elastically voice-and-chord strung,
tone's virtuoso, yet it is not song.
Laughter is difference and unity;
it swaps cultures as chickens cross roads,
yet the joke's not on Colonel Sanders
who laughs all the way to the Pentagon.
Laughter punctures megalomania
but is self-collapsing. In theatre, its regime
never fails, but life's its other standard.
The laughter of evil does not qualify;
parody of course, but sarcasm not.
The child is its natural habitat.

Teething Time

Was it in the bath ballooning bubbles,
or acting vagrant in vibrating grass,
you first discovered flotation magic
in the dunes and breeding swamps of childhood?
When did you first learn the arse-jolt lesson
that drifting on clouds could only happen
in a foreign niche in your head no eyes
can find, despite commiserating purrs
in your lap? So it was you built yourself
and friends an ark to ride out the questions,
and on their flood sail your pet theories
until you found an island of answers.
Next dawn, across cornflakes, neither mum nor dad
could savour the sweetmeats in the words you said ...

We are Reminded

We are reminded, each breakfast reminds
us, that we live our lives—their cornflakes, their
desserts—in between shifting beginnings
and quicksand ends. We are reminded, all,
all, all of us how that wandering
minstrel the sun sucks us in, spits us out.
We are reminded by the ludicrous
pretence of the frog, keeping glottal time
with the clock all night, how water darkness
is the lasting pool of contradiction.
We are reminded by opening hard
embossed covers of books by dead authors
that these may be coffin lids, may be last
exposures waxed in light of love's repast.

Demonising the Other

We live in an area-of-darkness
age in which premature deaths on the Chain
of Being abound. Try as you might to
avert your eyes, turn off your conscience switch,
screaming throes of pain invade black and white
sleep in which crimson is the colour not
of Love's rose but of bloodshed. Crusaders
and fanatics addicted to a fatal
embrace. Pacifists don't know where to turn,
bolting doors and windows in shacks of shock;
fabricating lives based on great texts, good
plans, working hard with grace of humour
civilised by haute cuisine, fine wine … as if
they're not the ones pushing others off the cliff.

Biting the Apple

To lavish on those we love some simple
secrecy of adoration, even though
as tongue-in-cheek whispering, yet interpreted
as a statement of the ultimate heart,
is a visceral hymn of passion play
which never declines the gifts of beauty
nor shuns compassion for those brutalised
lost ones robbed of their minds. So draw
lines in sand to exclude ruthless predators:
life's hypocrites devoid of conscience qualms
who set up the need to invent a god
for salvation's sake. But this Mystery
is but myth's apple on that Eden Tree,
and all cultures charge the same entry fee.

Anancy's Old Come-on Extravaganza

Notwithstanding my tongue exhibits words
which slide disarmingly along your thighs,
nor that my apostolic eyes are birds
(not the doves you expect, but cormorants
of lascivious desire), bewitch me
I beseech with Eros sighs; keep your heart
at a distance but always in reach.
Grant that and I shall play the lover's part
with profligate ardour. My bank account
is nocturnally eternally solvent,
my bone-flute music seductively flies
peripatetically through tropic
skies with a ripe ardour of rhetoric
which makes even the ghosts of ghouls love-sick.

À la Proust

Remembrance of a beachcomber boyhood's
spirally shells, quick crabs, salty surf spray
lingers even while the daydream's fading,
while its signifiers of the sixth sense
harvest the imagination's wheat-fields,
hang Picassos on labyrinthine walls,
stroll into Monet's garden to admire
the perfumed quietus of lilies floating …
Which reminds you how contra-melancholy
Debussy's resonant silences are
and yet how compatible bush music
of an easterly in the eucalypts;
how eerie the yellow innuendo,
grief-glorious, as wattles come and go.

Letting the Dog Back In

His eyes are weak, the blue and milkiness
of the sky are barely distinguishable:
Likewise these days the outlines of hills, wire
paddock fencing, quotation marks around
dialogue, low-tide wrinkles on the beach
where shells have been crunched by anonymous
feet; elusive sounds of the sea at night
drifting in and out of the mind's reaches
until scratching at the door reminds him
to let the curly-coated retriever
back in (and don't forget fresh water in
the bowl and the sacramental biscuit).
Tail-wagging says this dog has had her day:
keeping grunting koalas and roos at bay.

Fellow Traveller

Glib globe-trotter with a shoulder-slung bag,
drink in hand, he finds a terrace table
to write his news from Somewhere to Elsewhere.
In his address book he keeps a diary
in code—perfumed fragments, fleeting glances—
and his girlfriend's photo between pressed wild
flowers from Crete … And sensual excerpts
from wine-stained pages of Durrell's *Justine*.
Convinced that the largesse of odyssey
consists of having a bloody good time,
redolent with 'enlightenment and songs
of edifying experience' as
he writes, free from shame, in a letter home.
No mention, though, of last night's lover's name.

Immobilised by the Mobile

You are as curious and dedicated
a voyeur as the next man or woman
but the game has lost the sting in its tail.
Everywhere—bus and train routes, lavatories,
autumn canopied benches in courtyards,
lewd fingering under a café table,
in the midst (would you believe) of Wordsworth
tears; at the footy match, in a lecture
on *The Rime of the Ancient Mariner*,
the wholly sonorous masturbation
of Mass: such tribal needs for Show and Tell
now crave epiphanies on mobile phones;
senseless bravado without secrecy,
caricatures devoid of mystery.

Job Interview

Yes, I'm an Addict-for-the-Moment guy
and PARASITES GET LOST is my motto.
Yes, I know the dollar's sow and ripe-reap
ratio. *No,* I don't give a Judas-arse
fuck what the banks demand or what the source
of ill-gotten wealth is. My job's to make
it flow in our direction. My stripe-suit mate
with the holster bulge inside his jacket
is Gentle Smoking Joe. His accuracy's
legendary. Muck around with him, you're
on your way to the crematorium.
I see by your smile of satisfaction
you're pleased with my slick credentials spiel.
And, *Yes Sir!,* I can smell your golden deal.

Junior Mateship

When in the afternoon of high summer
and dissolving time a sea breeze gently
unlayers the past, you drift back into
awkward childhood's pink-faced embarrassments,
its pains, joys, frivolities; after-
dark larks that furrowed stern maternal brows;
the guilty hayshed hedonism perving
over illicit photos while quaffing
blackberry wine (we found the recipe
in Mrs Beeton). Adventure was all
despite our sunken boat, tree houses blown
away, the bike ride around the island that
never happened. Life was aromatic
as the *Craven A*'s smoked in the attic.

Aberrations

They appear like shadows not quite our own
mimicking dance-steps in a parody
play, or weird quirks of nature: Caliban
plotting revenge in his fetid lair, or
Ariel conjuring masques out of air;
bruises surfacing before the blow's struck;
flecks of self in one's offspring—they'll surprise
each self-conceit in your sea-dreaming eyes
and threaten peace in retirement's orchard
where the rugged-up elderly doze in chairs
under citrus, pear, plum and apple trees
as the sky's juices bloat clouds to thunder.
Then some sacrifice or tribute falls due
to void the ghost purporting to be you.

Summer Equinox

Drifting best describes the locomotion
of her phosphorescent feet at the flat
calm's lisping edge under the Aurora's
shafting brilliance, the astrological
surveillance of Venus, Mars, shooting stars
and the tilted Cross ('skylights of a
firmament lacking angels'). He follows
the blueprint of her footsteps up the beach
for love in the dunes in indigo air …
but there is more to it than that, so add
a tartan blanket to smother prickles,
a spray to disperse ants and mosquitoes,
an ice-bucket's bottle of chardonnay
and you've got coitus till the smudge of day.

Overcast Day

The wing of melancholia flicks at me ...
– Graham Greene

Even though I may be like every man
(woman too) in voicing opinions, I
don't want to be an adjudicator
either at a Rose Show or of the thorns
of mischief in the mind: enemy's, friend's,
loved one's, my own. Everyone's secrecies
in such matters deserve respect. Do you not
agree? Even though it may be the end
of the affair when you look too closely
into the heart of the matter, something
may still be deferred in places where
there is room to manoeuvre, honourably,
even in the departure lounge of life
where the lover is someone else's wife.

Hyphenation,
or 'Only connect'

Only connect the prose and the passion, and both
will be exalted, and human love will be seen at its height.
– E.M. Forster

Whatever you find in the front garden

or backyard of your language universe

don't ignore among fructuous roots and gems

of connection—sounds, vowels, letters, rules

of incestuous grammars—the short-straight-quick

hyphen, speech's great marriage-maker;

concordial, yet paradoxical

if needs be; avatar of sacred love,

like The Fairie Queen's, and coitus rapture

lyrics. So celebrate cross-gendering

hyphens, not just penis-shaped exclamation

marks or mammary brackets. Let desire

ignite to unite and parenthesis

envy the hyphen's copulating bliss.

Mirror Image

Espy him inspecting his eyes, his mouth,
his cross-bow smile in the gilt-framed mirror
and hope for one shivering second his
shadow cannot see you standing on it
in the soft pelt of carpet. Eye the knife,
metaphorically speaking, raised just
like an exclamation mark in your fist,
equipped for the executioner's role.
Then, mysteriously, the moment freezes
as if an independent judiciary
asks not how you plead but what's your motive,
and what explains the sorrow, the envy,
of this nightmare devil, this commonplace
mortality staring you in the face.

Just Desserts

He asks her what she thought about those wine-
crossed lovers in the Verona Café
cubicle. 'Whet my appetite,' she says.
'Well, did you notice their under-the-table
fondlings? And then the damp crotch patch when he
went to the loo? 'That's not the point,' she says,
her opulent finger in his left ear
while her other hand pianissimos
along his thigh urging him not to die
just yet. But he has nothing more to add
and focuses his undistracted will
on the choice of dessert. 'Anise ice-cream
perhaps?' 'Be daring', she says. 'Why not fig
with banana in armagnac? Think big!'

Affairs of the Blood

Staring at framed photos on the mantle
above the fireplace that's not been ablaze
for many a winter, the lineage of
five generations' transmigration through
black and white, sepia and colour prints,
see how fashions of the mask conceal affairs
of the blood and transmogrification,
how the stasis of the studio pose
imitates the silk-artificial rose.
And yet, quarter-moon smile here, averting
eye there, produce enigmatic effects
as of experience repressed, innocence
fading … the inherited glint of a gene
which rebels against conformity's routine.

The Pilgrim has a Glimmer or Two of Enlightenment

(for Jayashree and Srinath)

Back in Bangalore, Mysore, Manasa-
Gangotri, Dhvanyaloka's garden;
the spaciousness of hospitality
there where all who enter are novitiates
in a mercurial extended family.
Back from the highways in car and A-C
bus, the streets at all angles, the footpath
obstacle race where organized chaos
theory works in mysterious ways, he
numbers these among his luckiest, much
blessed of days. So what can he give in
return, and then only after he's come
back to a different likewise-postcard place,
with comparable conundrums of caste and race?

Beach Gallops:
Stanley, Tasmania

There's challenge in the sea's corrugations,
the torso's orchestralised pulse and beat,
to be met as acacias do the breeze
and porpoises the spasms of the waves.
Such are the prevailing conditions now
in the cemetery's grassed-down depression
between Bass Strait and 'The Nut' monolith
where butterflies flick and dab the blue air,
like paint-brushes, for eyes of ancestors,
from which deliquescence I, even now,
see with them again my mother's summer
(spent with her aunt in this fishing village),
galloping by waves and dunes down the coast:
grey mare, divining girl; a unified ghost.

Our National Game

(for Bruce Dawe and Brian Matthews)

No, not Real Estate! Not Pinot Tastings.
No, not morning-teas at imitation
Government Houses in spunk-and-spam streets
in Toorak, NOT reeking of blackbeard toast.
And no muddy soles on crème-de-la-crème
carpets at savvy soirées, at wife-swap
auctions in the cattle-yards of bourgeois
decorum under Cathedral shadows.
No, not who sucked whom in politic
réal chambers (how uncomfortable)
while mounting the spin that this was an all-
win confluence of virile best interests.
What bloody larks, eh? But they're not for me.
We're for Grand Finals at the M.C.G.

Winter's Tale

The difficulty of disappearance
is that you cannot rearrange your dreams
so that your life becomes real history.
But that only happens in books written
by others who feel free to tell you
what your dreams and stories meant. Like latter-day
soothsayers with problems in one hand but
swift solutions in the other. Arid
plains you look down on now from twisted peaks,
those ancient eruptions of cliff circled
by scavenging beaks, call into question
the impossible dream of Christian Thought
as if the resurrection is always
there, available to the end of Time's days.

Ode and Urn

The latest lantern in the dark aglow
drifts me back into the future's lost past.
Sins invisible, scents paradisal
reconnect floating fragments while these days'
emotions are not recollected in
Spartan tranquillity. Thus so much hurt's
harvested under the sunlight of lost
opportunities evoked by smells of
wisteria wafting down one wind, squashed
ants up another, and ancestral facts
after the carnage changing everyone's
fates. Like life, that is a problem poem
no-one knows how to end: no compromise
between pale-faced truth and beautiful lies.

A Rain Canticle

'Still falls the rain', so Edith Sitwell wrote
with liturgical solemnity. 'I
think continually of those who were
truly great', said Spender, informing Man's
world at large. 'Unreal city' was Eliot's
warning. Yet this poetic stuff of memory
still echoes in the gentle rain drifting
along our valley, dampening pages
of visionary modernism; its inks
bleeding slowly. Their turn now to wear old
hats. But this rain—their rain—is a purist
hymnal for those who believe in the true
believers. And when rain drops pock my face
I welcome insinuations of grace.

Romance

Nothing is more gentle than our poet
and his partner savouring a yoghurt
and muesli breakfast, sunlight seraphic
on the jug of orange juice, and Dino
Lupati's exhilarating Chopin
making love to the piano as if
even suburban romance can survive
in this quite miserable world we live in.
So let trust at least be redeemable
with his hand on his heart, kiss on her cheek;
intermingling sighs aromatic with
nectar spectrums in give and take gardens
where trysting configurations flower
from the first to the last sun-dial's hour.

Fencing Metaphor

(for Rick Hosking)

The wire stretches mystery's final length
which we test at sunrise: the usual
things, useless yet necessary, the lot
of the builder, the despair of his mate.
But what you must appreciate is skill,
the art of this: the scripture discipline
of post-hole perfection & the crucial
tool for stretching, for teasing the wrought mesh
until the enclosure's rooted, hammered
in place with arboreal lattice grace
where roses riotous as viruses
under the sun's microscope will keep
vigil while the eyes of state entrust
texts of treaties to survive, but not rust.

Dear Will,

Two loves I have of comfort and despair
entwined, neither able to give to each
other solstice solace or recompense,
nor share a compatible fruition;
their seasons being hemispherically
opposite, their gardens' prodigal worth
in inverse ratio to their bounties:
constituted thus they divide my earth.
But as you are text aplenty for all
the world—its truths and lies alike—
and such crises of heart and head, of pen
and word, as dreams are made on, vouchsafe me
safe passage between Scylla and Charybdis
home to the other side of paradise.

Bringing a Book to Life

(for Tully, Nena, Rick, Graham)

The more parents the better. For such birth
there's no dishonour, no pride in scandal
for being a collective progenitor
of an infant text that has multiple
mummies and daddies, and more siblings on
the way, and their closest elder ones long
gone to new homes in other diasporas
far-flung in polar and equatorial zones.
For Creation, after all, is incest
rampant, as are its languages, as are
its scripts, scrolls, accounts, histories, fictions,
ledgers, poems, receipts, circulating
voices—affirming, denying, conciliating—
in heads on pillows, in the bush warbling.

Time Warp

The father would be silently dismayed,
the mother vehemently mortified. That's
the way it was when transgression crossed swords
with purity over the breakfast porridge.
Morality was all! So were its blind
spots, crochet and meringue afternoon teas
which interrogated reputations
but not the pious past's moth-eaten sermons:
& yet how ennobling the creamy milk
of kindness, caresses like Chinese silk,
despite the jolt of the hanged suicide
in his cowshed; our war-hero, sports star,
depressed adulterer. So what use, then,
parables of bliss for all God's children?

No Sweat!

When yesteryear's truisms are always
tomorrow's anomalies and the bile
of circumstance here and now in this toy
TV video-manic town is spewing
sweat-stained singlet clichés…*love you baby*…
at sweet and sour white weddings and so, so
sad predictable funerals—what else
to say, save forget-me-knots on the grave?
Tomorrow was always too late to make
amends, to read the obituary
and suppress (of all things, churning
in your guts) Macbeth's ultimate statement.
Crows' cries copulate in the brass-hot sky,
out here, amid the breathless stubbled rye.

Scumbag in Uniform

I was not entertained nor overawed
by urinating bladder-skites or by
tedious would-be Olympic athletes
specialising in gob-spitting farthest
and farting loudest. Boy scouts sequestered
in tents buffeted by contrapuntal
weathers could be cruel, but the real scumbag
was the scout-master at the bus depot
in the wintry dark of late afternoon
who tapped an unsuspecting schoolboy's crotch.
Hiding under the umbrella's 'true grit
and spunk real men are made of' bullshit, he
was our flies' overlord: our stiff-moustached
enemy within who snarled as we marched.

Oedipus but not Rex

Every obsession needs its land's end
as you do now driving into the sun
blinding as it sets; the farm-strewn paddocks
loquacious with crows. Light is grain-golden
as tidal shadows are overlapping
your anxieties while you calculate
how late your arrival will be, yet how
premature your dawn departure. But your
secret's safe with me (or what's a conscience
for if not to perfect the double-cross?).
Your destination is log-booked, your fate
will ring the bell. The opening door wafts
perfume and roast lamb in your direction:
But where are you going, my son, my son?

The Ocean Child in Hobart Town, 1844

Must have been the name of a sailing ship
I guess. Clipper? Whaler? Convict transporter?
So benign seeming, anchored in the port
after the ravages of the Roaring
Forties; farming and leg-iron cargo
crumbling at the joints as sea-legs stutter
across cobble stones and the dire Saviour's
image under the frowning mountain,
sore with sunset, welcomes the arrivées
to, at last, this womb-forlorn resting place:
the hostelry a quarter-mile up-hill
bribing all and sundry with flaming hearth,
bread, fish, frothing ale. Hark the harp
cellar-resonant! Time's tunes: soft, wry, sharp.

I Get a Kick out of You

What would the voice of our youth be without
old reverberations of radio? …
the serial, not what you had for breakfast
but *The Search for the Golden Boomerang*
with the sad irony of its theme music …
the Hit Parade chaperoned by the Ink
Spots, *Danny Boy,* Al Jolson resurrected,
'I'm dreaming of a white Christmas', 'Goodnight
Sweetheart', and—in conscience space—Othello
singing for all time *Ol' Man River.* Where,
in what garden, slept you then when this sense
the meek call moral and the wise subtle
was morse-coded in slumber until day-
break when love in your arms is here to stay.

Creative Writing Gathering Hastings Bay (28.01.07)

(I.M. *Bruce Poulson*)

'Sift your stories', you said, 'for alluvial
symmetries'; archival facts that make sense
of fiction like the ministry of frost
attending the midnight ordination
of the offspring incandescent poem,
like 'surprises of the sun', the nightingale's
invention of extrasensory odes,
the paradox of the fortunate Fall.
Hence Milton's blind vision and Hemingway's
wounds of war to end all wounds were fuel
and grist for what and how you taught; the ghost
of the Word you met once in Stoke Poges,
and brought back home to revive history
and art and nurture the family tree.

From Penneshaw at Midnight

As I look out at this ocean of night
Infinity is a concept my mind
cannot comprehend—like spacelessness,
like timelessness—except in lieu of death.
Such falling-star metaphysics remind
me of those Atlantic mariners (less
than twenty average life-times ago)
staring sunsetwards to the horizon's
sheer precipice, imagining their frail
ship sinking like stone through endless air, all
their sins remembered in their orisons.
Trembling noviciates crossing chests then,
even now, as our full moon floods the sea;
our eastern sky in tune with mystery.

The Best is Yet to Come

(for Jaime)

Distressful as it is when time is out
of joint, and the brash world's a kangaroo
wilderness, and this petty pace from day
to day syndrome makes for dubious havoc
on the awkward stage of self-confidence:
this, however, is a time to plant, time
to fruit. Years as good as they get for, in
Yeats' words, 'the young in one another's arms'.
This is what I believe for you and us
and where we go from here, luscious with faith
and commitments: love's get-together of
past and present—like the tides, thresholds,
that embraced in first and last places long
ago, reincarnated in our song.

Triangles in the Sky

Migration is one first law of nature:
it's in the oceans and it's in the skies.
The evidence is before your eyes each
time you witness what we see between clouds
at night. Slow process lit up; death's spurting
brevity in a falling star's beauty.
Witness, too, native cockatoos, true to
the season's calendar, colonising
pine trees in a feasting frenzy as if
enough's never enough, and that is when
lovers lick the full moon's cream off the sea
and before they draw the curtains watch winged
triangular formations of herons flying
north, and we tremble, and you're crying.

Out There

The mists drift in and out of sight. Somewhere
nowhere, yet there in the shrouded paddocks
heart-beats are as prolific as light-beats
in the black sky, indifferent, absolute.
Yet wispishly there are what our tent flaps
open into: a resurrection dawn
of our camp-fire, the breakfast sizzling in
the pan while the world at large has coals for eyes.
Then it is you stumble into a rich kind
of reality where the collisions
of trigonometrical moths and insects
decorate the flypaper of your un-
folding life as you write or do not write
it down when mists drift in and out of sight.

Five Sonnets for Vincent O'Sullivan

(from RITES OF SPRING)

Poetry Interruptus

(On *reading* Nice Morning for It, Adam)

Knock, knock, a voice polite as silk softly
said, surprising the poem I was reading.

She held out a smiling plate of Asian
entrees that looked delicious, but which I

declined with banal gracelessness—'I have
just had lunch, I'm full': simple words, easy

to digest, yet even in the saying
I was shaken by my instinctive lie's

betrayal of that honourable stomach
where candour is stored, melliferous as

honey in a jar like the stanzas in
the book I was scanning when interrupted ...

knock, knock ... tune morsels for the inner ear
& the Poem-in-Waiting's pure idea.

'Not what skeletons think about'

You would endorse Wallace Stevens' remark,
'One day enriches a year', and perchance
apply it to your reading of Keats' Odes,
'The Sunne Rising', 'To his Coy Mistress', Bronte
wutherings; the 'endlessly rocking' 'cradle',
'the musical shuttle' of American
verse; of Thoreau going and coming 'with
a strange liberty in Nature, a part
of herself'; of poetry as 'the supreme
fiction'. Stevens at his westward window
watching shadows duelling in an autumn
wind; insurance executive with the eye
of a blackbird and thirteen directions
for flying to the bluest, freshest heavens.

On re-reading O'Sullivan's essay on Gwen Harwood

Artists are sometimes understood, well-judged
(although spasmodically—*aye, there's the rub*)
by practitioners of their mutual 'craft
and sullen art', but what truly bonds them
is deliciously vicious art for art's
sake wit. Thus soul-mate poets are inspired
by mutual respect, and also, yes,
envy, but of the non-satanic kind;
jealous awe suffused with joy and rapture.
And the kind of vigilant ironic
meta-wit with which Vincent assesses
Eisenbart's 'ripe waste of his heart's decay,
Too old to love, too young to die': 'making
love to a mistress who bored him rigid'.

On re-reading Gwen Harwood's
The Lion's Bride

I leave the patio—book, pad and Cooper's

Pale Ale—and enter the bird-burst garden

to witness a stump-grinder shattering

the base of an ancient palm, spewing mulch

back to the soil that had given it

life in the time-vague first place; however

you measure, quantify, the slow gentle

growth of fern, moss, vine, leaves, paper-wasp palm.

Returning to my chair I find the supple

breeze had wafted a loose page from *Selected*

Poems to the floor: an Oyster Cove homage

to James McAuley who would have chuckled

at this synchronicity of spirit,

'fountaining ... sap and hope' with mercurial wit.

In Debbie and Nigel's garden, Cairns, 25-09-06

Encore

Autumns on, trans-migrating wings return
with flight-and-glide beauty for the last time
to the nest where a quick generation
farewells drifting feathers and forgotten
bones, just as in a sunlit basinet
a pink finger feels the rough leather of
the hand of a great-grandmother's blood bond
moments before dark clouds erase the sun.
Encore, the west wind iterates, *encore,*
under the eaves of the house of the heart
and in the cavern of the pulsing ear
until—come the somersault of the year—
it's time for flittering wings to rehearse
the oldest journey in the sky of verse.

Dougie's ton

In memory of Greg Trott
(25/9/1934 – 5/3/2005),
who carried his bat with him.

Do you remember where you were when Doug

Walters smashed the six over mid-wicket

for the two tons-in-one-hit record? (I

was indolently tense fronting the black-

and-white TV in lime-green curtained light.)

Doug's genius for timing akin to

Pound's 'Make it new'; Eliot's *Observations;*

Our undefeated '48 side. We

swapped snap-shot memories of where we were

(in which front bar, wireless blaring) the day

the Gabba Test was tied; when JFK

died; how in Perth—Day Two, last ball—Dougie

clipped the red pill into a sky of fame

to immortalise his true-mateship name.

'As the last ball of the day was bowled Doug Walters was on ninety-seven.
He needed six for his century in the session and three for the round
hundred. The ball was short and Walters dispatched it for six over the mid-
wicket boundary as myriads of children swarmed onto the field to engulf
their hero.'   (Frank Tyson, *Test of Nerves*, p. 69)

'Between tea and stumps he had made exactly a hundred. A practical joker
himself, he returned expecting a hero's welcome, only to find the dressing
-room deserted. His colleagues were hiding in the showers.'
                    (Christopher Martin-Jenkins, *Assault on the Ashes*, p. 80)